The First Dinosaurs

The editors gratefully thank Claudia Berghaus, Diane Gabriel, and the Geology Section of the Milwaukee Public Museum for their enthusiastic cooperation and technical assistance. And thanks, too, to Matthew Peterson, second grader at Catholic East Elementary School in Milwaukee, for his invaluable assistance.

Library of Congress Cataloging-in-Publication Data

Burton, Jane.
  The first dinosaurs.

    (The New dinosaur library)
    "First published in The age of dinosaurs: a photographic record in the United Kingdom"--T.p. verso.
    Includes index.
    Summary: Brief text and illustrations introduce the characteristics and natural environment of thirteen early dinosaurs such as Saltopus and Dimetrodon. Includes a glossary of terms and miscellaneous facts about dinosaurs.
        1. Dinosaurs--Juvenile literature. [1. Dinosaurs] I. Kirk, Steve, ill. II. Dixon, Dougal. III. Title. IV. Series.
QE862.D5B84   1987   567.9'1   87-6460
ISBN 1-55532-283-2
ISBN 1-55532-258-1 (lib. bdg.)

This North American edition first published in 1987 by

Gareth Stevens, Inc.
7317 West Green Tree Road Milwaukee, WI 53223, USA

Design: Laurie Shock.
Background photography in selected photos: Norman Tomalin, Paul Wakefield, David Houston.
Photo retouching: Kay Robinson.
Line drawings: Laurie Shock and Paul Robinson.
Additional text: MaryLee Knowlton.
Series editors: MaryLee Knowlton & Mark J. Sachner.

Technical consultant: Diane Gabriel, Assistant Curator of Paleontology, Milwaukee Public Museum.

4 5 6 7 8 9 92 91 90 89 88

The First Dinosaurs

Photography by
Jane Burton

Text by
Dougal Dixon

Artwork of Photographed Reptiles by
Steve Kirk

Gareth Stevens Publishing
Milwaukee

THE NEW DINOSAUR LIBRARY

Hunting the Dinosaurs and Other Prehistoric Animals

The First Dinosaurs

The Jurassic Dinosaurs

The Last Dinosaurs

The First Dinosaurs

The Age of Dinosaurs goes back to 225 million years ago. But not all prehistoric animals were dinosaurs. Other reptiles appeared 345 million years ago and gave rise to the dinosaurs. Some of these prehistoric reptiles were tiny creatures like the little lizards we see today. Some were larger than any animals living now.

The first period of the dinosaurs lasted until 190 million years ago. By this time they ruled the Earth, and they would continue to rule for another 125 million years.

CONTENTS

HYLONOMUS

Hylonomus was one of the first *reptiles*. Unlike its *ancestors,* it laid its eggs on land. The young grew inside the leathery eggshell. They probably hatched fully developed. Hylonomus ate bugs. It would have had dry skin and a shape like lizards of today.

When Hylonomus lived, the forest was an endless swamp. As trees and plants decayed, they became coal. This took hundreds of millions of years.

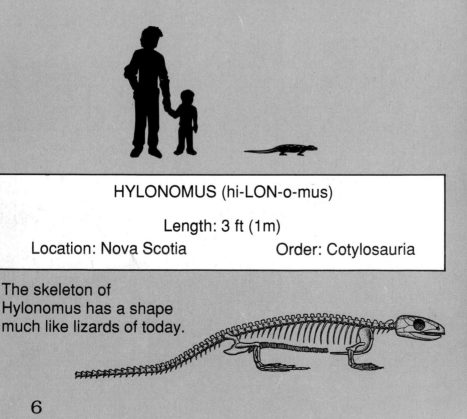

HYLONOMUS (hi-LON-o-mus)

Length: 3 ft (1m)

Location: Nova Scotia   Order: Cotylosauria

The skeleton of Hylonomus has a shape much like lizards of today.

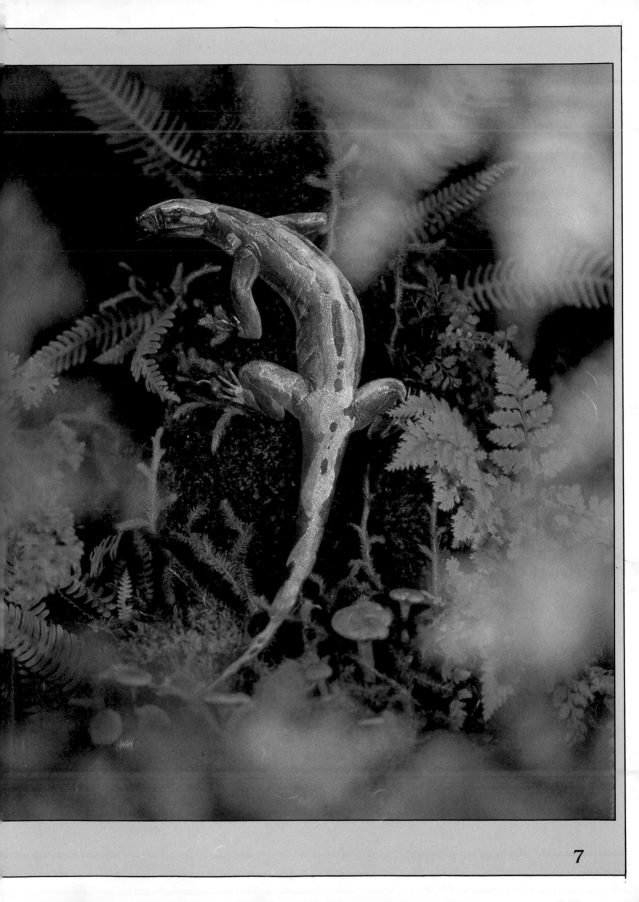

Edaphosaurus lived at the
same time as Dimetrodon. It
was similar in size and also
had a fin. It was a plant-
eater.

DIMETRODON

Dimetrodon looked like a large lizard with a sail on its back. This sail, or fin, may have soaked up heat from the sun. This heat would have warmed the rest of Dimetrodon's body. Other animals would wake up cold and sluggish. But Dimetrodon probably woke up warm, active, and hungry.

Dimetrodon was a meat-eater. Its teeth were long in front for attacking its *prey* and short in back for chewing. Dimetrodon was *cold-blooded*. But it was probably one of the first animals that could adjust its body temperature. This gave it an advantage over other animals.

DIMETRODON (di-ME-tro-don)

Length: 11 ft (3 m)

Location: Texas and Oklahoma   Order: Pelycosauria

LYCAENOPS

Lycaenops was an early *mammal*-like reptile. It had a body like dogs of today. The body was over the feet, instead of slung between them, so it could move faster. It had long killing teeth in front and slicing teeth in back.

Lycaenops and other mammal-like reptiles were the strongest, most active animals in their time. Some of the larger ones were as big as today's cows. These were usually plant-eaters. The smaller ones were active hunters.

LYCAENOPS (lie-KAY-nops)

Length: 3 ft (1 m)

Location: South Africa   Order: Therapsida

A mammal-like reptile such as Lycaenops (1) supported its body on top of straight legs. A lizard-like reptile like Pareiasaurus (2), also shown above, has legs that sprawl sideways.

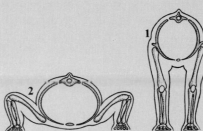

The skeleton of Cynognathus
looks like a dog, especially
its teeth and legs.

CYNOGNATHUS

Cynognathus was like today's mammals in many ways. It had hair. It was probably *warm-blooded*. It had mammal-like legs and teeth. The female may have nursed her babies.

But Cynognathus was still a reptile. Scientists say this because of its jaw. The jaw was still very primitive and typical of a reptile. It also probably could not hear well and probably still laid eggs, like other reptiles.

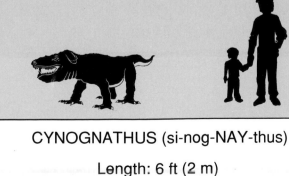

CYNOGNATHUS (si-nog-NAY-thus)

Length: 6 ft (2 m)

Location: South Africa   Order: Therapsida

LYSTROSAURUS

Most mammal-like reptiles were similar to each other. They had nearly the same shape and life habits. Lystrosaurus was different, though. It lived in water like today's hippopotamus. It was shaped like a barrel. It looked clumsy, but it was graceful in the water. Its legs could also support it on land. Lystrosaurus' nose and eyes were on top of its head. This way it could look around and breathe while hiding under water.

LYSTROSAURUS (lis-tro-SAW-rus)
Length: 3 ft (1 m)   Height at Shoulder: 19 in (50 cm)
Location: South Africa, India, and Antarctica
Order: Dicynodontia

Lystrosaurus remains have been found on three continents—evidence that these continents were once joined.

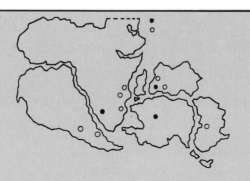

Proterosuchus had long hind
legs and a long tail. These
made walking on two feet
possible for its descendants,
the dinosaurs.

PROTEROSUCHUS

Like its *descendants,* the dinosaurs, Proterosuchus was an archosaur. At the time of Proterosuchus, archosaurs were reptiles that lived in the water. Proterosuchus had a long jaw, long body, powerful flattened tail, and strong hind legs. These features made it nicely suited to living and eating in the water.

These *aquatic*, or swimming, reptiles became the ancestors of dinosaurs that would walk upright on land. Crocodiles are descendants of archosaurs, too. So are pterosaurs, the flying reptiles.

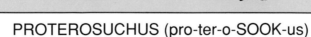

PROTEROSUCHUS (pro-ter-o-SOOK-us)

Length: 5 ft (1.5 m)

Location: Africa   Order: Thecodontia

PODOPTERYX
and
LONGISQUAMA

Podopteryx and Longisquama may have been ancestors of later flying animals. Sitting on a branch, they looked like tree lizards.

Skin attached to Podopteryx's legs helped it sail like a glider. Longisquama had a crest of long scales on its back. They were V-shaped, and they could be folded across its back. These scales were probably an early form of feathers.

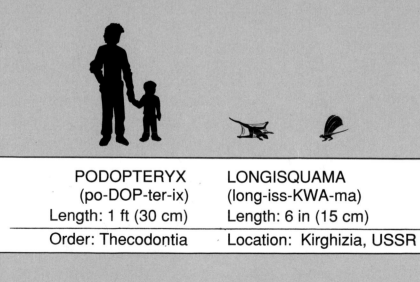

PODOPTERYX	LONGISQUAMA
(po-DOP-ter-ix)	(long-iss-KWA-ma)
Length: 1 ft (30 cm)	Length: 6 in (15 cm)
Order: Thecodontia	Location: Kirghizia, USSR

Another flying reptile:
Kuehneosaurus. Its wings
were formed by extensions of its ribs.

This is a complete adult
nothosaur skeleton with
two babies.

NOTHOSAURUS
and
TANYSTROPHEUS

Nothosaurus was a long-toothed swimming reptile. It had the beginnings of paddle-like feet and a fin on its tail. Its teeth were *adapted* for catching fish.

Tanystropheus had a very long neck — 10 ft (3 m). This probably helped it reach fish in rockpools. At first the only remains found were neckbones. Because these bones were so long, *paleontologists* thought they were legs.

NOTHOSAURUS (no-THO-saw-rus)	TANYSTROPHEUS (tan-iss-TRO-fee-us)
Length: 10 ft (3m)	Length: 13 ft (4 m)
Order: Sauropterygia	Order: Protorosauria
Location: England, Israel,	Location: southwest Poland
the Netherlands, Jordan, India, Japan, China	

SALTOPUS

Saltopus was a tiny dinosaur, built like a chicken. It walked on its back legs and used its front legs like hands to catch food. Like its ancestors, it had five fingers on each hand. But it only used three. In animals that arose after Saltopus, the fourth and fifth fingers disappeared.

Saltopus ate smaller animals like Morganucodon, one of the earliest mammals. Morganucodon was much like today's shrew. This early mammal remained unchanged through the 150 million year reign of the dinosaurs.

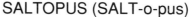

SALTOPUS (SALT-o-pus)

Length: 2 ft (60 cm)   Length at hips: 8 in (20 cm)

Location: Scotland   Order: Saurischia

Saltopus was a
procompsognathid, an
early, primitive meat-eater.
In the early 1800s,
procompsognathid footprints
were found in the Connecticut
River Valley. Discoverers first
thought they were *fossil* bird
tracks.

This Hyperodapedon skull
shows the beak and the double
row of teeth at the back of the jaw.
The lower jaw is not shown.
Its one row of teeth fit between
the two top rows. The teeth were
like scissors slicing food.

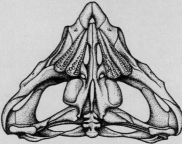

HYPERODAPEDON

Hyperodapedon was a plant-eater. It may have died out when the plant life changed from soft green plants to trees in its homeland.

Hyperodapedon had a beak to nip off plants. It also had two rows of back teeth in its upper jaw and one row in the lower jaw that fit between the two top rows.

Hyperodapedon was related to today's tuatara of New Zealand. The tuatara is the only survivor of the order Rhynchocephalia.

HYPERODAPEDON (hi-pare-o-DAP-ih-don)

Length: 4 ft (1 m)

Location: Scotland   Order: Rhynchocephalia

THECODONTOSAURUS

Thecodontosaurus was *omnivorous*. Like its ancestors, it ate meat. But it was also among the first dinosaurs to eat plants. Many dinosaurs would *evolve* into plant-eaters. As this happened, they became much larger.

Thecodontosaurus could walk on two or four legs. Many of its footprints have been found. This may mean that it traveled in herds. It also may have *migrated* each year. In the rainy season, it lived in the hills. In the dry season, it came down from the hills to the warmer plains.

THECODONTOSAURUS (thee-co-dont-o-SAW-rus)

Length: 6 ft (2m)   Order: Saurischia

Location: England and possibly
South Africa and Australia

Thecodontosaurus was a prosauropod (2),
eating both meat and plants. Its ancestors were
thecodonts (1), meat-eaters. Its descendants
were sauropods (3), plant-eaters.

Fun Facts About Dinosaurs

1. Here are some animals that lived with the first dinosaurs and still survive today:

    > starfish, horseshoe crabs, clams, oysters, squid
    > coelacanths
    > cockroaches
    > dragonflies
    > lungfish
    > tuataras
    > ants

2. It is impossible to know exactly what color dinosaurs must have been. As with animals of today, the color of dinosaurs probably depended on their habitat and sex. Also like animals of today, the dinosaurs were probably mostly green and brown in color, since these colors would have helped them hide among plants or rocks.

3. The definition of a reptile includes laying eggs. Since all dinosaurs were reptiles, most scientists feel that all dinosaurs laid eggs. This has not always been easy to prove, however. Eggs are very fragile, so few have survived as fossils. Also, because the fossils of some newly born dinosaurs are so big, some scientists wonder about the possibility of live births.

4. Plant-eating dinosaurs had teeth that could grind their food, and some had a horny beak for nipping off plants. Some plant-eaters had several rows, or batteries, of teeth — often up to 2,000 in their mouth at one time. Also, unlike humans, who come with only two sets of teeth, all dinosaurs had continuous tooth replacement.

5. Meat-eating dinosaurs had very strong jaws and sharp teeth that could rip flesh from their prey. Usually meat-eaters were very fast, so they could catch fleeing animals. Or they were very strong and had vicious claws.

6. In Triassic times, when the first dinosaurs lived, the continents we know today were one large land mass called Pangaea, which means "all earth."

7. A cold-blooded flesh-eating dinosaur would eat its body weight in food in 60 days. A warm-blooded animal would eat its body weight in six to ten days.

8. Like dinosaurs, crocodiles came from thecodonts, 200 million years ago.

9. Feathers are *modified* scales that probably developed as *insulation* to control the body temperature.

10. All the mammal-like reptiles died out by the end of the Triassic period.

11. Poland has a series of postage stamps with pictures of dinosaurs and other reptiles like Dimetrodon.

12. The jellyfish was one of the first animals with a mouth and a stomach.

13. The animals that we call dinosaurs are actually two subgroups of the group called Archosauria. These two subgroups are Ornithischia, which means "bird-hipped," and Saurischia, which means "lizard-hipped." Both groups include some dinosaurs that walked on two feet and some that walked on four feet. Both groups also include meat-eaters and plant-eaters. The division of dinosaurs into Ornithischia or Saurischia is based on the types of pelvis or hips they have.

14. Both dinosaurs and pterosaurs, which were flying and gliding reptiles, belonged to the group Archosauria. The crocodile of today is also an archosaur.

More Books About Dinosaurs

Here are some more books about dinosaurs and other animals of their time. If you see any you would like to read, see if your library or bookstore has them.

About Dinosaurs. Morris (Penguin)
The Age of Dinosaurs! Parker (Gareth Stevens)
Dinosaurs. Jackson (National Geographic Society)
Dinosaurs and Other Archosaurs. Zallinger (Random House)
Dinosaur Time. Parish (Starstream Products)
Hunting the Dinosaurs and Other Prehistoric Animals. Burton /
    Dixon (Gareth Stevens)
The Jurassic Dinosaurs. Burton / Dixon (Gareth Stevens)
The Last Dinosaurs. Burton / Dixon (Gareth Stevens)
Sea Monsters: Ancient Reptiles that Ruled the Sea. Eldridge
    (Troll)

New Words

Here are some new words from *The First Dinosaurs*. They appear for the first time in the text in *italics*, just as they appear here.

adapted .... changed to fit new needs
ancestors .... animals from which other animals have evolved
aquatic .... living, growing, or swimming in the water
cold-blooded .... an animal unable to control its body temperature
descendants .... animals that evolved from earlier types of animals

evolve .... to develop by adapting and changing to suit changing environments

fossil .... the remains or traces of a plant or animal. Fossils are preserved in sedimentary rock formations. Sedimentary rocks are rocks that are laid down in water.

insulation .... protection from heat or cold

mammal .... one of the groups of vertebrates, or animals with a backbone. Mammals have live babies and nurse their young. They do not lay eggs. They are warm-blooded and have only two sets of teeth —milk or baby teeth and permanent teeth. Mammals are often furred or have hairy skin. Cats, whales, horses, and human beings are mammals.

migrated .... moved from one place to another

modified .... changed in form

omnivorous
(om-NIV-er-us) .... eating a varied diet of plants, meat, insects, and eggs

paleontologists
(pay-lee-on-TOL-o-gists) ..... scientists who study fossils

prey .... an animal killed for food by another animal

reptile(s) .... an animal that lays its eggs encased in shells on land. Reptiles have horny skin or scales. They are cold-blooded. Lizards, snakes, and crocodiles are reptiles.

warm-blooded .... an animal able to control its body temperature

Index and Pronunciation Guide

Note: The use of a capital letter for an animal's name means that it is a specific *type,* or *genus,* of
32 animal—like a Saltopus or Dimetrodon. The use of a lower case, or small, letter means that it is a
member of a larger *group* of animals—like archosaurs or pterosaurs.